THE CREATION

IN FULL SCORE

JOSEPH HAYDN

Dover Publications, Inc., New York

This Dover edition, first published in 1990, is a republication
of *Die Schöpfung*, originally published by C. F. Peters, Leipzig, n.d.
The foreword has been translated into English,
and a list of instruments has been added.

Manufactured in the United States of America
Dover Publications, Inc.
31 East 2nd Street
Mineola, N.Y. 11501

Library of Congress Cataloging-in-Publication Data

Haydn, Joseph, 1732–1809.
[Schöpfung. English & German]
The Creation.

Oratorio in 3 parts.
For solo voices (SSTBB), mixed chorus, and orchestra.
English and German words.
Text based on portions of: Paradise lost / John Milton.
Reprint. Originally published: Die Schöpfung.
Leipzig : C. F. Peters, 18—.
1. Oratorios—Scores.   I. Swieten, Gottfried van, 1734–1803.
II. Milton, John, 1608–1674. Paradise lost.   III. Title.
M2000.H35S34   1990   90-751179
ISBN 0-486-26411-4 (pbk.)

CONTENTS

FIRST PART

SECOND PART

THIRD PART

FOREWORD

The original Viennese score from the year 1800 served as the model for the editing of this work. Since, however, aside from numerous engraver's errors, many inaccuracies were found there with respect both to execution and to performance, this new edition contains several departures from the original score:

1. The double-bass part has been provided with notes in the higher octave in passages where it lies too low.
2. In the B♭-horn parts, the words *alto* and *basso* have been added in the appropriate passages.
3. In the 3rd-trombone part, small notes have occasionally been added for practical performance reasons.

Page 7, measure 10. The natural signs beside the A's, lacking in the original score, have been added here, since an F-minor chord after the words "there was light" and "that it was good" could hardly have been conceived by Haydn.

Page 103. In the original score, parallel octaves occur between the penultimate and last measures:

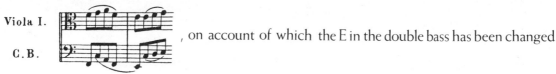

, on account of which the E in the double bass has been changed to the C above.

Page 118. The performance markings *p* and *ff* are only found in the original score at the repetition on page 122. The word *cresc.* has been added.

Page 127, last measure. The *p* in the original score has here been changed to *f*.

Page 178, measure 2. The original score shows: 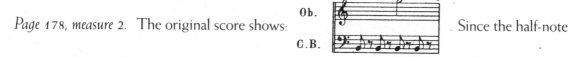 . Since the half-note rest before the G is lacking here, a whole-note may have been intended instead of the half-note, and has been provided in this edition. (In the original score, whole-notes always appear in the *middle* of the measure.)

Page 204. In the original score, the timpani has not 4 but 5 downbeat quarter-note G's, and only then comes the ♩♪♪♩ | ♩ 𝄾 | figure; this has been changed here.

Page 244, measure 3, 2nd quarter-note. In the original score, a C appears in both the 2nd trombone and the 2nd violins; because of the parallel fifths, these notes were changed to B♭'s.

THE CREATION
[Die Schöpfung]

Oratorio in three parts
Text by Gottfried, Baron van Swieten
Music by Joseph Haydn
First public performance: Vienna, 19 March 1799

CHARACTERS AND VOICES

Raphael	Bass
Uriel	Tenor
Gabriel	Soprano
Eve	Soprano
Adam	Bass

INSTRUMENTATION

3 Flutes [Flauto, Fl.]
2 Oboes [Ob.]
2 Clarinets (B♭, C) [Clarinetto in B, C; Clar.]
2 Bassoons [Fagotto, Fag.]
Contrabassoon [Contrafagotto, Contraf., C. Fag.]
2 Horns (B♭ basso, C, D, E♭, E, F, A, B♭ alto)
[Corni in B basso, C, D, Es, E, F, A, B alto]
2 Trumpets (B♭, C, D) [Clarini in B, C, D]
3 Trombones [Tromb.]
Timpani [Timp.]
Violins I, II [Violino, Viol.]
Violas
Cellos [Vcello, Vcll]
Basses [Basso, C.B.]
Basso Continuo (with Harpsichord [Cembalo])

ERSTER THEIL.

1. EINLEITUNG.

Die Vorstellung des Chaos.

8

2. ARIE mit CHOR.

Nun schwanden vor dem hei - - li-gen Strahle des schwarzen Dunkels gräuli-che Schatten.
Now va-nish before the ho - - ly beams the gloo - my dismal shades of dark.

Nun schwanden vor dem hei - - li-gen Strahle des schwarzen Dunkels gräuliche Schatten;
Now va-nish before the ho - - ly beams the gloo - my dismal shades of dark.

Vcello.

CB. unis.

der er-ste Tag ent-stand; der er-steTag ent-stand.
the first of days ap-pears; *the first of days ap-pears.*

Verwirrung weicht, und
Dis-or-der yields, to

Vcl.
CB.

Ord - nung, und Ord - nung keimt em - - por.
or - der to or - der fair the place.

Verwirrung weicht.
Dis-or-der yields,

Verwirrung weicht, und Ord - nung
Dis-or-der yields to or - der

unis.

keimt em-por, und Ord- - nung keimt em-por.
fair the place, to or- -der fair the place.

Allegro moderato.

Er-starrt ent-flieht der Höl-len-gei - ster Schaar, in des Ab - grunds Tie - fen hin-
Af-frighted fled hell's spi-rits black in throngs, *down* *they sink* *in the deep* *of a-*

CB.

Allegro moderato. Vcello.

Mezza voce.

Und ei-ne neu-e Welt, und ei-ne neu-e Welt ent-springt, ent-springt auf Got-tes
And new cre-a-ted world, a new cre-a-ted world springs up, springs up at God's com-

Und ei-ne neu-e Welt, und ei-ne neu-e Welt ent-springt, ent-springt auf Got-tes
And new cre-a-ted world, a new cre-a-ted world springs up, springs up at God's com-

Und ei-ne neu-e Welt, und ei-ne neu-e Welt ent-springt, ent-springt auf Got-tes
And new cre-a-ted world, a new cre-a-ted world springs up, springs up at God's com-

Und ei-ne neu-e Welt, und ei-ne neu-e Welt ent-springt, ent-springt auf Got-tes
And new cre-a-ted world, a new cre-a-ted world springs up, springs up at God's com-

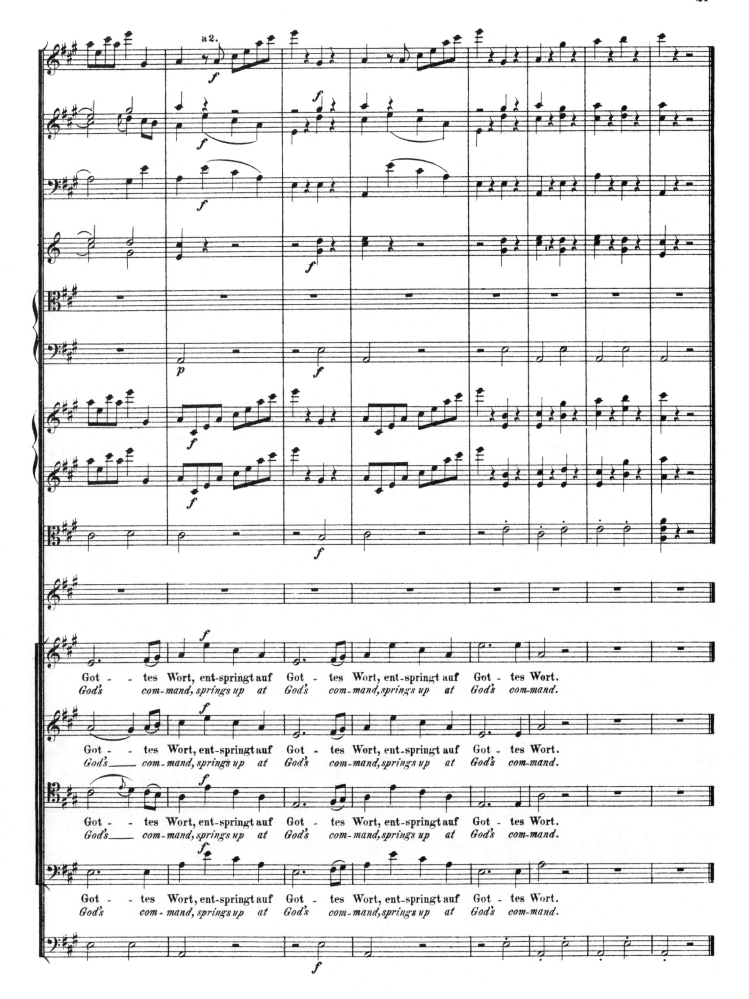

Got - - - tes Wort, ent-springt auf Got - - tes Wort, ent-springt auf Got - tes Wort.
God's com-mand, springs up at God's com-mand, springs up at God's com-mand.

Got - - - tes Wort, ent-springt auf Got - - tes Wort, ent-springt auf Got - tes Wort.
God's com-mand, springs up at God's com-mand, springs up at God's com-mand.

Got - - - tes Wort, ent-springt auf Got - - tes Wort, ent-springt auf Got - tes Wort.
God's com-mand, springs up at God's com-mand, springs up at God's com-mand.

Got - - tes Wort, ent-springt auf Got - - tes Wort, ent-springt auf Got - tes Wort.
God's com-mand, springs up at God's com-mand, springs up at God's com-mand.

3. RECITATIV.

Flauto I. II.

Oboe I. II.

Clarinetto I. II. in C.

Fagotto I. II.

Timpano in C.

Violino I.

Violino II.

Viola.

Raphael.

Und Gott machte das Fir-ma-ment, und theil-te die Was-ser, die un-ter dem Fir-ma-ment
And God made the fir-ma-ment, and di-vi-ded the wa-ters, which were un-der the fir-ma-

Cembalo.

Violoncello e Basso.

Allegro assai.

wa-ren, von den Ge-wässern, die o-ber dem Firmament wa-ren, und es ward so.
ment, from the wa-ters, which were a-bove the fir-ma-ment. and it was so.

f Allegro assai

Wie Spreu vor dem Win-de, so flo-gen die Wol-ken.
As chaff by the winds are im-pel-led the clouds.

Die Luft durchschnitten feu-ri-ge Bli-tze,
By hea-vens fire the sky is en-fla-med,

und schrecklich rollten die Don-ner um-her.
and aw-full rolled the thunders on high.

Vcello.

C B. *ff*

Vcello.

C.B.

I^{mo}

a 2.

Der Fluth entstieg auf sein Ge-heiss der all-er-
Now from the floods in steams as-cend re-vi-ring

Cembalo.

unis

qui - cken - de Re - gen,
sho - wers of rain,

der all ver - hee - ren - de
the drea - ry waste - ful

Violino I.

Violino II.

Viola.

RAPHAEL.

Schauer,
hail,

der leich - te flo - cki - ge Schnee.
the light and fla - - ky snow.

Basso.

attacca

4. CHOR mit SOPRAN SOLO.

Stau-nen sieht das Wun-derwerk   der Himmelsbürger   fro - - - he   Schaar,   und
marv'lous work be-holds a-maz'd   the glo - rious   hie-rar-chy of   heav'n,   and

laut ertönt aus ih - ren Kehlen   des Schöpfers Lob.   des Schöpfers Lob.   das Lob des zwei-ten
to th'ethereal vaults re-sound   thr praise of God.   the praise of God.   and of the se-cond

Tags, das Lob des zwei-ten Tags.
day, and of the se - cond day.

Und laut ertönt aus ih - ren Keh-len   des Schöpfers

And to th'ethe-real vaults re - sound   the praise of

Und laut ertönt aus ih - ren Keh-len   des Schöpfers

And to th'ethe-real vaults re - sound   the praise of

Staunen sieht das Wunderwerk der Himmels - bür - ger fro - he Schaar. und laut
mar'lous work be - holds amaz'd the glorious hie - rarchy of heav'n, and from th'e-the-real vaults

und laut er - tönt des Schöpfers

and from and from th'ethe-real

und laut er - tönt des Schöpfers

and from and from th'ethe-real

er - tönt des Schö-pfers Lob, das Lob des zwei - ten Tags.

re-sound the praise of God, and of the se - cond day.

Mit

The

Lob, das Lob des zwei-ten Tags, das Lob des zwei - ten Tags.

vaults re-sound the praise of God, and of the se - cond day.

Lob, das Lob des zwei - ten Tags, das Lob des zwei - ten Tags.

vaults re-sound the praise of God, and of the se - cond day.

das Lob des zwei - ten Tags. Und laut_____
and of the se - cond day. And from th'e-the-real vaults_____

Lob, das Lob des zwei - ten Tags, das Lob des zwei-ten Tags. Und laut, und laut er-tönt des Schöpfers
God, and of the se - cond day, and of the se-cond day. And from the vaults, and from th'e- the-real

Lob, das Lob des zwei - ten Tags, des zwei-ten Tags. Und laut, und laut er-tönt des Schöpfers
God, and of the se - cond day, the se-cond day. And from the vaults, and from th'e-the-real

Lob, das Lob des zwei-ten Tags, des zwei-ten Tags. Und laut, und laut er-tönt des Schöpfers
God, and of the se-cond day, the se-cond day. And from the vaults, and from th'e-the-real

5. RECITATIV.

6. ARIE.

Rol - - - lend in schäu - - - menden Wel - len be - wegt sich
Rol - - - ling in foa - - - ming bi - lows up - lift - - - ed

un - - ge-stüm das Meer.   Rol - lend in schäu-menden Wel - len be -
roars the boist' - rous sea.   Rol - ling in foa - ming bil - lows up -

wegt sich, be - wegt sich un - gestüm das Meer, be - wegt sich un - gestüm das
lift - ed, up - lift - - ed roars the boist'-rous sea, up - lift - ed roars the boist-rous

Meer.
sea.

Hü - gel und Fel - sen er-schei - nen, der Ber - ge
Mountains and rocks now e - merge, their tops in - -

Gi - pfel steigt em - por,   der Ber - ge Gi - pfel steigt em - por.
to   the clouds as - cend,   their   tops   in - to   the   clouds   as - cend.

Hü - gel und Fel - sen er - scheinen,   der Ber-ge Gi-pfel steigt   em - por, der Ber-ge Gi - pfel steigt em -
Mountains and rocks now e - merge,   their tops in - to the clouds   as - cend, their tops in - to   the clouds as -

por, der Ber - ge Gi - - pfel steigt em - por.
cend, their tops in - - to the clouds as - cend.

SOLI.

SOLO.

tacet.

Die Flä - che, weit ge - dehnt, durchläuft der brei - te Strom in man - cher
Thro' th'o - pen plains out - stretch - ing wide in ser - pent er - ror ri - vers

43

der brei - te Strom _____ in mancher Krüm - - - - - me.
er - ror ri - vers flow, _____ ri - vers flow. _____

Lei - - se rau - - schend glei - - tet fort, im
Soft - - ly pur - - ling glides on, thro'

Bach.
brook.

Lei - - se rau - - schend glei - - tet fort, im
Soft - ly pur - ling glides on thro'

stil - - len Thal der hel - le Bach;
si - - lent vales the lim - pid brook;

lei - - se
soft - - ly

7. RECITATIV.

Gabriel.

Cembalo.

Und Gott sprach: Es brin - ge die Er-de Gras her - vor. Kräu-ter, die Sa-men
And God said: *Let the earth bring forth grass,* *the herb yiel-ding*

Basso.

ge - ben, und Obst-bäu - me die Früch - te brin - gen ih - rer Art ge - mäss,
seed and the fruit-tree yiel-ding fruit af - - ter his kind

die ih - ren Sa-men in sich selbst ha-ben auf der Er - de, und es ward so.
whose seed is in it-self u - -pon the earth, and it was so.

8. ARIE.

Andante.

Flauto I II.

Clarinetto I in B.

SOLO.

Fagotto I II.

I. SOLO.

Corni in B alto.

Violino I.

Violino II.

Viola.

Gabriel.

Nun beut die Flur das fri-sche Grün dem
With ver-dure clad the fields ap-pear de-

Violoncello e Basso.

Andante.

hier sprosst den
here shoots the

Wun - den Heil, _____ den Wun - den Heil, _____ hier sprosst den Wun - den
hea - ling plant, _____ *the hea - ling plant,* _____ *here shoots the kea - ling*

Fl. a 2.
Clar.
Fag. a 2.
Cor.

Heil. Die Zwei - ge krümmt der gold - nen Früch-te Last.
plant. *By load of fruits th'ex - pan-ded boughs are press'd;*

9. RECITATIV.

Uriel.

Und die himmlischen Herr - schaaren verkün - digten den dritten Tag, Gott prei - send und sprechend:
And the hea - ven - ly host proclai - med the third day, praising God and say - ing:

Cembalo.

Basso.

54

10. CHOR.

sang erschal - len! Froh - lo - cket dem Herrn, dem mäch-tigen Gott! Frohlo - cket dem Herrn, dem mäch - ti-gen

voi - - ces raise! In tri - umph sing the migh - ty Lord! In tri - umph sing the migh - ty

sang erschal - len! Froh - lo - cket dem Herrn, dem mäch-tigen Gott! Frohlo - cket dem Herrn, dem mäch - ti-gen

voi - - ces raise! In tri - umph sing the migh - ty Lord! Froh - lo - cket dem Herrn, dem
In tri - umph sing the

Er - de be -klei - det in herr - li-cher Pracht.
earth — has clo - thed in sta - te-ly dress.
Denn er hat Him - mel und
For he the hea - vens and

klei - det in herr - li-cher Pracht.
clo - thed in sta - te-ly dress.
Denn er hat Him - mel und
For he the hea - vens and
Er - de be-klei - det in
earth — has clo - thed, has

Him - mel und Er - de be - klei-det, denn er hat Him - mel und Er - de be - klei - det in herr - li-cher
hea - vens and earth — has clo - thed, for he the hea -vens and earth has clo - thed in sta - te - ly

Denn er hat Him - mel und Er - de be-klei - det in herr - li-cher Pracht.
For he the hea - vens and earth — has clo - thed in sta - te - ly dress.

stimmt an die Sai-ten,   ergreift die Leyer!   Froh - lo - cket dem Herrn,   dem mäch-ti-gen Gott!
a - wake the harp,   *the lyre a-wake!*   *In tri - umph sing*   *the migh - ty Lord!*

stimmt an die Sai-ten,   ergreift die Leyer!   Froh - lo - cket dem Herrn,   dem mäch-ti-gen Gott!
a - wake the harp,   *the lyre a`-wake!*   *In tri - umph sing*   *the migh - ty Lord!*

stimmt an die Sai-ten,   ergreift die Leyer!   Froh - lo - cket dem Herrn,   dem mäch-ti-gen Gott!
a - wake the harp,   *the lyre a-wake!*   *In tri - umph sing*   *the migh - ty Lord!*

stimmt an die Sai-ten,   ergreift die Leyer!   Froh - lo - cket dem Herrn,   dem mäch-ti-gen Gott!
a - wake the harp,   *the lyre a-wake!*   *In tri - umph sing*   *the migh - ty Lord!*

Denn er hat Him - mel und Er - de be - klei - det in herr - - - - - -
For he the hea - vens and earth has clo - thed in sta - - - - - -

Denn er hat Him - mel und Er - de be - klei - det in herr - li - cher Pracht,_____
For he the hea - vens and earth has clo - thed in sta - te - ly dress,_____

Denn er hat Him - mel und Er - de be - klei - det in herr - li - cher Pracht, in herr - -
For he the hea - vens and earth has clo - thed in sta - te - ly dress, in sta - -

Denn er hat Him - mel und Er - de be - klei - det in herr - li - cher Pracht, in herr - - -
For he the hea - vens and earth has clo - thed in sta - te - ly dress, in sta - -

- - - - - - - - - - - li-cher Pracht, in herr-li-cher Pracht.
- - - - - - - - - - - *te-ly dress, in sta-te-ly dress.*

in herr - - - li-cher Pracht, in herr - li-cher Pracht.
in sta - - - te-ly dress, in sta-te-ly dress.

- - - - - - - - - - - li-cher Pracht, in herr - li-cher Pracht.
- - - - - - - - - - - *te-ly dress, in sta-te-ly dress.*

- - - - - - - - - - - li-cher Pracht, in herr - li-cher Pracht.
- - - - - - - - - - - *te-ly dress, in sta-te-ly dress.*

11. RECITATIV.

Uriel. Und Gott sprach: Es sei'n Lich-ter an der Fe-ste des Himmels, um den
And God said: Let there be lights in the fir-ma-ment of hea-ven, to di-

Cembalo. / Basso.

Tag von der Nacht zu scheiden, und Licht auf der Er - de zu geben, und es sei'n die-se für Zeichen und für
vide the day from the night and to give light up-on the earth, and let them be for signs and for

Zei-ten und für Ta-ge und für Jah-re. Er mach-te die Ster-ne gleichfalls.
sea-sons and for days and for years. He made the stars al-so.

12. RECITATIV.

Andante. a2.

Flauto I.II. — pp — cresc. — ff
Oboe I.II.
Fagotto I.II.
Contrafagotto.
Corni in D.
Clarini in D.
Timpani in D.A.
Violino I.
Violino II. — pp
Viola. — pp cresc. f ff
Uriel.
Violoncello e Basso. — Violonc. pp unis. CB. Vcl. f ff

Andante.

Più Adagio.

pp

pp

pp

a tempo *mezza voce* pp

Bahn.
course.

Mit leisem Gang und sanf-tem Schimmer schleicht der Mond die stil - le Nacht hin-
With softer beams and mil-der light steps on the sil - ver moon thro' si - - - lent

Più Adagio.

pp senza Cembalo

Allegro.

f

p

f

f

p

f

Recit.

Cembalo

durch.
night.

Den aus-gedehn-ten Him-melsraum ziert oh - ne Zahl der hel-len Ster-ne Gold
The space immense of th'a-zur sky in-num'rous host of radiant orbs a-dorns,

Allegro. f

b?

und die Söhne Gottes ver-kündig-tenden vierten Tag mit himmlischem Ge-sang, sei-ne Macht aus rufend al - so:
and the sons of God an-noun-ced the fourth day in song di - vine proclai-ming thus his power.

13. CHOR mit SOLI.

seiner Hände Werk   zeigt an das Firma - ment,   und seiner Hände   Werk   zeigt

wonder of his works   displays the fir-ma-ment.   The   wonder of his   works   dis-

seiner Hände Werk   zeigt an das Firma - ment,   und seiner Hände Werk   zeigt

wonder of his works dis - plays the fir-ma-ment.   The wonder of his works   dis -

Violonc. e Basso.

Welt er-geht das Wort, jedem Ohre klingend, keiner Zunge fremd, keiner, keiner, kei - ner
lands re - sounds the word, never unper - cei - ved ever under-stood, ever, ever, ev - er

Wort, jedem Ohre klingend, keiner Zunge fremd, keiner, keiner, kei - ner
word, never unper - cei - ved ever under-stood, ever, ever, ev - er

geht das Wort, jedem Ohre klingend, keiner Zunge fremd, keiner, keiner, kei - ner
sounds the word. never unper - cei - ved ever under-stood, ever, ever, ev - er

pizz.   arco

Più Allegro.

keiner, kei - ner,___ kei - ner Zun - ge fremd.
ever, ev - er,___ ev - er un - der - stood.

keiner, kei - ner, kei - ner Zun - ge fremd.
ever, ev - er, ev - er un - der - stood.

keiner, kei - ner, kei - ner Zun - ge fremd.
ever, ev - er, ev - er un - der - stood.

Die Him - mel er - zäh - len die Eh - re___
The hea - vens are tel - ling the glo - ry of

Die Him - mel er - zäh - len die Eh - - re
The hea - vens are tel - ling the glo - ry of

CORO.

Die Him - mel er - zäh - len die Eh - re___ Got - tes, und
The hea - vens are tel - ling the glo - ry of God,___ the

Die Him - mel er - zäh - len die Eh - re___ Got - tes, und
The hea - vens are tel - ling the glo - ry of God,___ the

Più Allegro.

Got - tes, und sei-ner Hän-de Werk, und sei-ner Hän-de Werk zeigt an das Fir-ma - ment.
God,_____ the wonder of his works, the wonder of his works dis - plays the fir-ma - ment.

Got - tes, und sei-ner Hän-de Werk zeigt an, zeigt an das Fir-ma - ment.
God,_____ the wonder of his works dis - plays, dis - plays the fir-ma - ment.

sei - ner, und sei-ner Hän-de Werk zeigt an, zeigt an das Fir-ma - ment.
won - der, the wonder of his works dis - plays, dis - plays the fir-ma - ment.

sei - ner, und sei-ner Hän-de Werk, und sei-ner Hän-de Werk zeigt an das Fir-ma - ment.
won - der, the won-der of his works, the won-der of his works dis - plays the fir-ma - ment.

Und seiner Hände Werk___ zeigt an das Firma - ment, das Firma - ment.
The wonder of his works___ dis - plays the firma - ment, the firma - ment.

Und seiner Hände Werk zeigt an das Firma - ment. Und seiner
The wonder of his works dis - plays the firma - ment. The wonder

ment, das Firma-ment. Und seiner Hände Werk zeigt
ment, the firma - ment. The wonder of his works dis -

ment. Und seiner HändeWerk zeigt an, zeigt
ment. The wonder of his works dis-plays, dis -

Und seiner Hände Werk zeigt an das Firma-ment, das Firma - ment.
The wonder of his works dis - plays the firma - ment, the firma - ment.

Hände Werk zeigt an das Firma-ment.
of his works dis - plays the firma - ment.

Und seiner Hände Werk ___ zeigt an das
The wonder of his works ___ dis-plays the

an das Fir - ma - ment. Und seiner Hände Werk, zeigt an das Firma - ment. Und seiner Hände Werk zeigt
plays the fir - ma - ment. The wonder of his works dis - plays the firma - ment. The wonder of his works dis -

an das Fir - ma - ment. Und seiner Hände Werk, und seiner Hände Werk zeigt an das Fir - ma -
plays the fir - ma - ment. The wonder of his works, the wonder of his works dis - plays the fir - ma -

84

ment   Und sei - ner   HändeWerk zeigt   an   das Fir - ma -ment.   Und   seiner Hände
ment.   The won-der   of his works dis - plays the fir - ma -ment.   The   wonder of his

HändeWerk —— zeigt   an,   zeigt   an das Fir - ma -ment.   Und   seiner Hände
of his works—— dis - plays,   dis - plays the fir - ma -ment.   The   wonder of his

seiner HändeWerk zeigt an das Fir - ma - ment,das Firma - ment.   Und
and the wonder of   his works dis-plays, dis - plays the fir - ma - ment.   The

an   das Fir - ma - ment,————— das Firma - ment.   Und   seiner Hände
plays   the fir - ma - ment,————— the fir - ma - ment.   The   wonder of his

Eh - - re Gottes, und seiner Hände Werk zeigt an das Firma-ment, zeigt an das Firma-ment, zeigt
glo - ry of God, the wonder of his works dis - plays the firma - ment, dis - plays the firma - ment, dis-

zäh - len die Eh - - re Got - tes, und seiner Hände Werk zeigt an das Firma-
tel - ling the glo - - ry of God, the wonder of his works dis-plays the firma -

- - re Got - tes, und seiner Hände Werk zeigt an das Firma-ment, zeigt an das Firma-ment, zeigt
ry of God, the wonder of his works dis - plays the firma - ment, dis-plays the firma - ment, dis -

Eh - - re Got - tes, und seiner Hände Werk _____ zeigt an, _____ zeigt an _____
glo - ry of God, the wonder of his works _____ dis - plays, _____ dis - plays, _____

ff

ment, zeigt an das Fir - ma - ment, zeigt an das Firma-ment, zeigt an das Firma - ment.
ment, dis - plays the fir - ma - ment, dis-plays the firma - ment, dis - plays the firma - ment.

Werk zeigt an das Fir - ma - ment, zeigt an das Firma-ment, zeigt an das Firma - ment.
works dis - plays the fir - ma - ment, dis-plays the firma - ment, dis - plays the firma - ment.

— zeigt an das Fir - ma - ment, zeigt an das Firma-ment, zeigt an das Firma - ment.
— dis - plays the fir - ma - ment, dis-plays the firma - ment, dis - plays the firma - ment.

an das Fir - ma - ment, zeigt an das Firma-ment, zeigt an das Firma - ment.
plays the fir - ma - ment, dis-plays the firma - ment, dis - plays the firma - ment.

Ende des ersten Theils.

ZWEITER THEIL.
14. RECITATIV.

Und Gott sprach:
And God said:
Es brin - ge das
Let the wa - ters bring

Was - ser in der Fül - le her - vor we - ben - de Ge - schöpfe, die Le - ben
forth a - bun - dant - ly the mo - ving creature, that has

ha - ben, und Vö - gel, die ü - ber der Er - de flie - gen mö - gen
life, and fowl, that may fly a - bove the earth

in dem of - fe - nen Fir - ma - men - te des Himmels.
in the o - pen fir - ma - ment of hea - ven.

15. ARIE.

noch war zur Kla-ge nicht ge-stimmt
nor to a mourn-ful tale were tun'd

ihr reizender,
her soft,

ihr
her

Fl.

Clar.

Corni.

rei-zender Ge-sang,
soft enchanting lays,

ihr rei - - - - -
her soft_____

Vcello.

Fl.

zender, ihr
en - chant - ing, her

unis.

16. RECITATIV.

Mehret euch, ihr Fluthenbe _ wohner, und fül _ let je _ de Tie _ fe! Seid fruchtbar, wachset,
Multi _ ply, ye fin _ ny tribes, and fill each watry deep. Be fruitful, grow and

(divisi)

meh _ ret euch! Er _ freu _ et euch in eu _ rem Gott, er _ freu _ et euch in eu _ rem Gott!
mul _ ti _ ply! And in your God and Lord re _ joice. and in your God and Lord re _ joice!

17. RECITATIV.

Recit.

Raphael.

Und die En _ gel rühr _ ten ihr' un _ sterb _ li _ chen
And the an _ gels struck their im _ mor _ tal

Cembalo.

Basso.

Har _ fen, und san _ gen die Wunder, und san _ gen die Wun _ der des fünf _ ten Tag's.
harps and the wonders, the won _ ders of the fifth day sung.

18. TERZETT.

110

attacca

19. CHOR mit SOLI.

gross | in seiner Macht, | und e - - wig bleibt sein Ruhm, | und
great, | *and great his might.* | *his glo - - ry lasts for e - ver,* | *for*

gross | in seiner Macht, | und e - - wig bleibt sein Ruhm, | und
great, | *and great his might.* | *his glo - - ry lasts for e - ver,* | *for*

in seiner Macht, | und e - wig bleibt und e - - wig bleibt sein Ruhm. | und
and great his might. | *his glo - ry lasts, his glo - - ry lasts for e - ver,* | *for*

e - - wig. | e - - wig bleibt sein Ruhm, | und
lasts, his glo - ry lasts for e - ver, | *for*

e - - wig, | e - - wig bleibt sein Ruhm, | und
lasts, his glo - ry lasts for e - ver, | *for*

e - - wig. | e - - wig bleibt sein Ruhm, | und
lasts, his glo - ry lasts for - ver, | *for*

e - - wig, | e - - wig bleibt sein Ruhm, | und
lasts, his glo - ry lasts for e - ver, | *for*

123

und e-wig bleibt _____ sein Ruhm, bleibt sein Ruhm. _____
his glo-ry lasts _____ *for e - ver, and e - - ver more.*

Ruhm, und e-wig bleibt _____ sein Ruhm, bleibt sein Ruhm. _____
more, his glo-ry lasts for e - ver, and e - - ver more.

Ruhm, und e-wig bleibt _____ sein Ruhm. _____
more, his glo-ry lasts, _____ and e - - ver more.

Ruhm, und e - - wig bleibt sein Ruhm. _____
more, for e - - ver, for e - ver, and e - - ver more.

Ruhm, und e - - wig bleibt sein Ruhm. _____
more, for e - - ver, for e - ver, and e - - ver more.

20. RECITATIV.

21. RECITATIV.

Das zackge Haupt er-hebt der schnelle Hirsch.
The nimble stag bears up his branching head.

Mit flie-gender Mäh-ne springt und wiehrt voll Muth und Kraft das ed_le Ross.
With fly_ _ing ma_ne and fie-ry look, im_pa-tient neighs the spright-ly steed.

Andante.

Fl.

Viol. I. pizz.

Viol. II. pizz.

Viola. pizz.

arco

arco

arco

Auf grü-nen Matten weidet schon das Rind, in
The cattle in herds al_ready seeks his food on

pizz.

pizz.

arco

arco

Andante.

Heerden ab - getheilt.
fields and meadows green.
Die Triften deckt, als wie ge - sät, das wollen-
And o'er the ground, as plants, are spread the fleecy,

rei - che, sanf - te Schaaf. Wie Staub ver - - breitet sich in Schwarm und Wir - bel das Heer der In - sek - ten
meek and blea - ting flock. Un-numberd as the sands in whirl a - rose the host of insects.

In lan - gen Zü - gen kriecht am Bo - - den das Ge - würm.
In long di - mensions creeps with si - nuous trace the worm.

22. ARIE.

Nun scheint in vol - lem Glan - ze der Himmel.
Now heav'n in ful - lest glo - ry shone;

Nun prangt in ih - - rem Schmu - cke die Er - de.
earth smiles in all her rich at - tire.

Die Luft er - füllt das leich - te Ge - fieder, die
The room of air with fowl___ is fill'd, *the*

Dem Gan - zen fehl - te das Ge - schöpf, das Got - tes Wer - - ke, dank - bar sehn,
There wan - ted yet that wondrous be - ing, that grate - ful should Gods pow'r ad - mire,

des Her - - ren Gü - - te prei - - sen soll.
with heart and voice his good - ness praise.

Doch war noch
But all the

23. RECITATIV.

Uriel.

Und Gott schuf den Menschen nach sei-nem E-ben-bil-de. Nach dem E-ben-bil-de
And God cre-a-ted man in his own i-mage. In the i--mage of

Cembalo.

Basso.

Got-tes schuf er ihn. Mann und Weib er-schuf er sie. Den A-them des
God cre-a-ted he him. Male and fe-male cre-a-ted he him. He breath--ed

Lebens hauchte er in sein An-gesicht und der Mensch wur-de zur le-ben-di-gen See-le.
in--to his nostrils the breath of life, and man be-came a li-ving soul.

24. ARIE.

Mit Würd' und Ho - heit an - ge - than, mit
In na - tive worth and ho - nour clad, with

ver - kündt der Weis - heit tie - fen Sinn,   und aus dem hel - len
of   wis - dom deep de - clares the seat,   and   in   his eyes with

Bli - - cke strahlt   der Geist,   des Schö - pfers Hauch und E - - ben - bild.
bright - - ness shines   the soul,   the breath and i - mage of his God.

Und aus dem hel - len Bli - - cke
And in his eyes with bright - - ness

Vcello.

Basso.

strahlt der Geist, des Schö - - pfers Hauch und E - - ben-bild.
shines the soul, the breath and i - - mage of_____ his God.

Vcello. e Basso.

144

25. RECITATIV.

Raphael.

Und Gott sah je - des Ding, was er gemacht hat - te; und es war sehr
And God saw ev'-ry thing, that he had made; and be-hold it was ve-ry

Cembalo.

Basso.

gut; und der himmli-sche Chor fei-er-te das En-de des sechsten Ta-ges mit lau-tem Gesang.
good; and the hea-ven-ly choir in song di-vine, thus closed the sixth day.

26. CHOR.

Flauto I.II.

Oboe I.II.

Fagotto I.II.

Corni in B basso.

Clarini in B.

Timpani in B.F.

Trombone I.II.

Trombone III e Contrafagotto.

Violino I.

Violino II.

Viola.

Soprano.

Alto.

Tenore.

Basso.

Violoncello e Basso.

146

Auch unsre Freud' er-schal - le laut, erschal - - - - - - - le
In lof-ty strains let us re-joice, in lof - - - - - ty strains let us re-

Auch unsre Freud' er-schal - le laut, erschal-le laut, auch unsre Freud'erschal-le laut, erschalle
In lof-ty strains let us re-joice, let us re - joice, in lof-ty strainslet us re-joice, let us re-

schal - le laut, auch unsre Freud' erschal - le laut, er-schal - le laut!
us re-joice, in lof-ty strains let us re - joice, let us re - joice!

laut, erschalle laut, auch unsre Freud' erschal - - - - - le
joice, let us rejoice, in lof-ty strains let us re - joice, let us re-

Vcello.

unis.

Lob sei un-ser Lied, sei un-ser Lied, sei un-ser Lied!   Auch uns-re Freud'   erschalle laut. Des Her-ren
be the praise of God, the praise of God, the praise of God!   *In lof-ty strains.*   *let us rejoice! Our song let*

des Her-ren Lob sei un-ser Lied, sei un-ser Lied!   Auch uns-re Freud'   erschalle laut. Des Her-ren
our song let be the praise of God, the praise of God!   *In lof-ty strains*   *let us rejoice! Our song let*

des Her-ren Lob sei un-ser Lied, sei un-ser Lied!   Auch uns-re Freud'   erschalle laut. Des Her-ren
our song let be the praise of God, the praise of God!   *In lof-ty strains*   *let us rejoice! Our song let*

des Her-ren Lob sei un-ser Lied, sei un-ser Lied!   Auch uns-re Freud'   erschalle laut. Des Her-ren
our song let be the praise of God, the praise of God!   *In lof-ty strains*   *let us rejoice! Our song let*

152

un-ser Lied, sei un - ser Lied!
praise of God, the praise of God!

un-ser Lied, sei un - ser Lied!
praise of God, the praise of God!

un-ser Lied, sei un - ser Lied!
praise of God, the praise of God!

un-ser Lied, sei un - ser Lied!
praise of God, the praise of God!

Attacca.

27. TERZETT.

Attacca.

28. CHOR.

denn er al - lein, denn er al - lein ist hoch er-ha - ben, ist hoch er - ha - ben, al - le - lu -
He sole on high ex-alt-ed reigns, he sole on high ex-alt - - ed reigns, al - le - lu -

ja, denn er al - lein, denn er al - lein ist hoch er - ha - ben, ist hoch er - ha - ben, al - le - lu -
ja, he sole on high ex-alt-ed reigns, he sole on high ex-alt-ed reigns, — al - le - lu -

ja,
ja,

Al - les lo-be sei-nen
Glo - ry to his name for

ja,
ja,

Vcello.

ja, al-le-lu-ja.   Al - - les lo-be sei-nen Na - - men,   al-le-lu-ja,
ja, al-le-lu-ja.   Glo - - ry to his name for ev - - - er,   al-le-lu-ja,

ja, al-le-lu-ja.   Al - - les lo-be sei-nen Na - - men,   al-le-lu-ja,
ja, al-le-lu-ja.   Glo - - ry to his name for ev - - - er,   al-le-lu-ja,

ja, al-le-lu-ja.   Al - - les lo-be sei-nen Na - - men,   al-le-lu-ja,
ja, al-le-lu-ja.   Glo - - ry to his name for ev - - - er,   al-le-lu-ja.

ben, al-le-lu-ja,   al-le-lu-
____ al-le-lu-ja,   al-le-lu-

168

Denn er al - lein __ ist hoch er - ha - ben, ist hoch er - ha - ben, __ al - le - lu - ja, al - le - lu -

ja. *He sole on high* __ *ex - alt - ed reigns,* *ex - alt - ed reigns,* __ *al - le - lu - ja, al - le - lu -*
ja.

ja. Denn er al - lein __ ist hoch er - ha - ben, ist hoch er - ha - - ben, al - le - lu -
ja.

ja. *He sole on high* __ *ex - alt - ed reigns,* *ex - alt - ed reigns,* __ *al - le - lu -*
ja.

ja, al - le - lu - ja. Al - les lo - be sei - nen Na - - men, denn er al - lein ist
Glo - ry to his name for ev - - er, he sole on high ex -

ja, al - le - lu - ja.
Denn er al - lein ___ ist hoch er - ha - ben,
He sole on high ___ ex - alt - ed reigns,

ja, al - le - lu - ja. Al - les lo - be sei - nen Na - - men, denn er al - lein ist
Glo - ry to his name for ev - - er, he sole on high ex -

ja, al - le - lu - ja.
Denn er al - lein ist hoch er - ha - ben,
He sole on high ex - alt - ed reigns,

hoch er-ha-ben, ist hoch er-ha-ben, al - le - lu - ja, al - le - lu - ja.
alt - - ed reigns, ex-alt-ed reigns, al - le - lu - ja, al - le - lu - ja.

ist hoch er-ha-ben, ist hoch er-ha-ben, al - le - lu - ja, al - le - lu - ja.
ex-alt-ed reigns, ex-alt-ed reigns, al - le - lu - ja, al - le - lu - ja.

hoch er-ha-ben, ist hoch er-ha-ben, al - le - lu - ja, al - le - lu - ja.
alt - - ed reigns, ex-alt-ed reigns, al - le - lu - ja, al - le - lu - ja.

ist hoch er-ha-ben, ist hoch er-ha-ben, al - le - lu - ja, al - le - lu - ja.
ex-alt-ed reigns, ex-alt-ed reigns, al - le - lu - ja, al - le - lu - ja.

Ende des zweiten Theils.

DRITTER THEIL.

29. RECITATIV.

Recit.

Aus Rosen-
ht

30. DUETT und CHOR.

183

Pflan - zen, duf - tet, Blu - men, haucht ihm eu - ern Wohl - ge - ruch.
plants ex - hale, ye flow - ers breathe at him your bal - my scent.

Ihr
Ye

Fl.

Ob.

Fag.

a 2.

Pflan - zen, duf - tet, Blu - men, haucht ihm eu - ern Wohl - ge - ruch!
plants ex - hale, ye flo - wers, breathe at him your bal - my scent.

ADAM.

Ihr, de - ren
Ye, that on

Pfad die Höh'n erklimmt, und ihr, die niedrig kriecht, ihr, de - ren Flug
mountains sta - tely tread and ye that low - ly creep, ye, ye birds, that sing

C.B.

Vcello.

unis.

Aus dei - nem Wort ent-stand die Welt; dich be - ten Erd' und Him - mel

Thy word call'd forth this won - d'rous frame. Thy pow'r a - dore the heav'n and

Aus dei - nem Wort ent-stand die Welt; dich be - ten Erd' und Him - mel

Thy word call'd forth this won - d'rous frame. Thy pow'r a - dore the heav'n and

prei - - sen dich wir prei-sen dich in E - - - wig-keit,
praise thee now, we praise thee now and ev - - - er more,

preisen dich in E - wig-keit, in E - - -wig-keit, in E -
praise thee now and ev - er more, and ev - - - er more, and ev -

keit, in E - wig-keit, wir prei-sen dich in
more, and ev - - er more, we praise thee now and

E - wigkeit, in E - wig-keit, wir prei-sen dich in E - wig-keit,
ev - ermore, and ev - er more, we praise thee now and ev - er more,

prei-sen dich in E - - - - - - - - wig - keit.

praise thee now and ev - - - - - - - - er more.

prei-sen dich in E - - - - - - - - wig - keit.

praise thee now and ev - - - - - - - - er more.

E - wigkeit, wir preisen dich in E - wigkeit, in E - wigkeit, in

ev - er more, we praise thee now and ev - er more, and ev - - er more, and

E - wigkeit, wir preisen dich in E - wigkeit, in E - wigkeit, in

ev - er more, we praise thee now and ev - er more, and ev - - er more, and

a 2.

Erd' und Him-mel an, wir prei-sen dich in E- -wig-keit, in E- -wig-

dore the heav'n and earth, we praise thee now and ev- -er more, and ev- -er

an, wir prei-sen dich, wir prei-sen dich in E- -wig-keit, in E- -wig-

earth, we praise thee now, we praise thee now and ev- -er more, and ev- -er

keit, in E - wig - keit.

more, and ev - er more.

keit, in E - wig keit.

more, and ev - er more.

31. RECITATIV.

Adam.

Nun ist die er-ste Pflicht er - füllt, dem Schöpfer haben wir gedankt. Nun fol-ge
Our du-ty we per-for-med now, in off'-ring up to God our thanks. Now follow

mir, Ge-fährtin meines Lebens! Ich lei - te dich, und je-der Schritt weckt neu-e Freud' in uns'rer
me, dear partner of my life! Thy guide I'll be, and ev'-ry step pours new delights in - to our

Brust, zeigt Wunder ü-ber-all. Er - ken-nen sollst du dann, welch un-aussprechlich Glück der Herr uns zu-ge-
breast, shew's wonders ev'-ry-where Then may'st thou feel and know the high de-gree of bliss, the Lord al-lotted

dacht, ihn preisen immerdar, ihm weihen Herz und Sinn. Komm, komm, folge mir, fol-ge mir! ich lei te dich!
us, and with de-vo-ted heart his boun-ty ce - le - brate. Come, come, follow me, follow me! thy guide I'll be.

Eva.

O du, für den ich ward! Mein Schirm, mein Schild, mein All! Dein Will' ist mir Gesetz.
O thou, for whom I am! My help, my shield, my all! Thy will is law to me.

Andante.

So hat's der Herr be - stimmt, und dir ge-hor-chen,
So God, our Lord, or - dains, and from o - be-dience,

und dir ge - hor - chen   bringt mir Freu - - - de, Glück und Ruhm
and from o - be - dience   grows my pride _____ and hap - pi - ness.

32. DUETT.

Die Küh - le des A - bends, o wie er-quicket sie !
The coolness of ev'n, o how she all restores !

Fl.

SOLO.

Wie rei-zend
How pleasing

Wie - la - bend ist der runden Früchte Saft !
How gra-te-ful is of fruits the sa-vour sweet !

SOLI.

ganz ge-weiht.
whole shall be.

ganz ge-weiht.
whole shall be.

Der thau-en-de Mor-gen, o wie ermuntert er!
The dew-dropping morn, o how she quickens all!

Die Küh-le des A-bends, o wie er-quicket sie!
The cool-ness of ev'n, o how she all restores!

sie:
new;

mit dir, mit dir ist Se - ligkeit das Le - ben;
with thee, with thee is li - fe in - cessant bliss,

sie;
new;

mit dir, mit dir ist Se - ligkeit das Le - ben;
with thee, with thee is li - fe in - cessant bliss,

dir, dir sei es ganz_____ ge - weiht.
thine, thine, thine it whole_____ shall be.

dir, dir sei es ganz_____ ge - weiht.
thine, thine, thine it whole_____ shall be.

33. RECITATIV.

34. SCHLUSSCHOR (mit SOLI.)

Lasst zu Eh - ren sei - nes Namens Lob in Wett-gesang er - schal - - - -len.

Ce - le-brate his pow'r and glo-ry. Let his name resound on high! _____

Lasst zu Eh - ren sei - nes Namens Lob in Wett-gesang er - schal - - - -len.

Ce - le-brate his pow'r and glo-ry. Let his name resound on high! _____

keit. A - - - - men. Des Herren Ruhm, er bleibt in E - wigkeit.
aye. A - - - - men The Lord is great, his praise shall last for aye.

Ruhm, er bleibt in E - wigkeit. Des Herren Ruhm, er bleibt in E - wigkeit.
great, his praise shall last for aye. The Lord is great, his praise shall last for aye.

- men, a - men, a - - - - - men. Er bleibt in E - wigkeit.
- men, a - men, a - - - - - men. his praise shall last for aye.

- men, a - men, a - men, a - - - - - men. Er bleibt in E - wig -
- men, a - men, a - men, a - - - - - men. his praise shall last for

Vcello.
unis.

keit. A - - - - - men. Des Her-ren Ruhm, er bleibt in E - wig
aye. A - - - - - men. The Lord is great, his praise shall last for

men, a - - - - men.
men, a - - - - men.

keit, in E-wig-keit. Des Her-ren Ruhm, er bleibt in E - wig-
aye, shall last for aye. The Lord is great, his praise shall last for

Des Her-ren Ruhm, er bleibt in E - wig-keit. A - - - -
The Lord is great, his praise shall last for aye. A - - - -

unis.

keit. A - men, a - - men, a - - men.
aye. A - men, a - - men, a - - men.

Des Herren Ruhm, er bleibt in E - wig - keit. Des Herren Ruhm, er
The Lord is great, his praise shall last for aye. The Lord is great, his

keit. A - - men. Des Herren Ruhm, er bleibt in E - wig - keit. Des Herren
aye. A - - men. The Lord is great, his praise shall last____ for aye. The Lord is

men. Des Herren Ruhm, er bleibt in E - wig - keit. A - - - men. Des Herren
men. The Lord is great, his praise shall last for aye. A - - - men. The Lord is

A - - - men. Des Herren Ruhm, er bleibt in E - wigkeit. A -
A - - - men. The Lord is great, his praise shall last for aye. A -

bleibt in E - wigkeit. A - men, a - - men, a - - men,
praise shall last for aye. A - men, a - - men, a - - men,

Ruhm, er bleibt in E - wigkeit, in E - wigkeit. A - men. a - men,
great, his praise shall last for aye, shall last for aye. A - men, a - men,

Ruhm, er bleibt in E - wigkeit. Des Herren Ruhm, er bleibt in
great, his praise shall last for aye. The Lord is great, his praise shall

keit,   er   bleibt,   er   bleibt   in   E - wig - keit,   singt dem
aye,   his   praise,   his   praise shall last   for aye,   sing the

keit,   er   bleibt,   er   bleibt   in   E - wig - keit,   singt dem
aye,   his   praise,   his praise shall last   for aye,   sing the

keit,   er   bleibt,   er   bleibt   in   E - wig - keit,   singt dem
aye,   his   praise,   his praise shall last   for aye,   sing the

keit,   er   bleibt,   er   bleibt   in   E - wig - keit,   singt dem
aye,   his   praise,   his   praise shall last   for aye,   sing the

Herren   al-le Stimmen!   Des Herren Ruhm, er bleibt in   E - wigkeit. A - men. A - men.
Lord   ut-ter thanks!   The Lord is great, his praise shall last   for aye. A - men. A - men.

Herren   al-le Stimmen!   Des Herren Ruhm, er bleibt in   E - wigkeit. A - men. A - men.
Lord   ut-ter thanks!   The Lord is great, his praise shall last   for aye. A - men. A - men.

Herren   al-le Stimmen!   Des Herren Ruhm, er bleibt in   E - wigkeit. A - men. A - men.
Lord   ut-ter thanks!   The Lord is great, his praise shall last   for aye. A - men. A - men.

Herren   al-le Stimmen!   Des Herren-Ruhm, er bleibt in   E - wigkeit. A - men. A - men.
Lord   ut-ter thanks!   The Lord is great, his praise shall last   for aye. A - men. A - men.

ENDE.

Dover Orchestral Scores

Bach, Johann Sebastian, COMPLETE CONCERTI FOR SOLO KEYBOARD AND ORCHESTRA IN FULL SCORE. Bach's seven complete concerti for solo keyboard and orchestra in full score from the authoritative Bach-Gesellschaft edition. 206pp. 9 x 12. 0-486-24929-8

Bach, Johann Sebastian, THE SIX BRANDENBURG CONCERTOS AND THE FOUR ORCHESTRAL SUITES IN FULL SCORE. Complete standard Bach-Gesellschaft editions in large, clear format. Study score. 273pp. 9 x 12. 0-486-23376-6

Bach, Johann Sebastian, THE THREE VIOLIN CONCERTI IN FULL SCORE. Concerto in A Minor, BWV 1041; Concerto in E Major, BWV 1042; and Concerto for Two Violins in D Minor, BWV 1043. Bach-Gesellschaft editions. 64pp. 9⅜ x 12¼. 0-486-25124-1

Beethoven, Ludwig van, COMPLETE PIANO CONCERTOS IN FULL SCORE. Complete scores of five great Beethoven piano concertos, with all cadenzas as he wrote them, reproduced from authoritative Breitkopf & Härtel edition. New Table of Contents. 384pp. 9⅜ x 12¼. 0-486-24563-2

Beethoven, Ludwig van, SIX GREAT OVERTURES IN FULL SCORE. Six staples of the orchestral repertoire from authoritative Breitkopf & Härtel edition. *Leonore Overtures,* Nos. 1–3; Overtures to *Coriolanus, Egmont, Fidelio.* 288pp. 9 x 12. 0-486-24789-9

Beethoven, Ludwig van, SYMPHONIES NOS. 1, 2, 3, AND 4 IN FULL SCORE. Republication of H. Litolff edition. 272pp. 9 x 12. 0-486-26033-X

Beethoven, Ludwig van, SYMPHONIES NOS. 5, 6 AND 7 IN FULL SCORE, Ludwig van Beethoven. Republication of H. Litolff edition. 272pp. 9 x 12. 0-486-26034-8

Beethoven, Ludwig van, SYMPHONIES NOS. 8 AND 9 IN FULL SCORE. Republication of H. Litolff edition. 256pp. 9 x 12. 0-486-26035-6

Beethoven, Ludwig van; Mendelssohn, Felix; and Tchaikovsky, Peter Ilyitch, GREAT ROMANTIC VIOLIN CONCERTI IN FULL SCORE. The Beethoven Op. 61, Mendelssohn Op. 64 and Tchaikovsky Op. 35 concertos reprinted from Breitkopf & Härtel editions. 224pp. 9 x 12. 0-486-24989-1

Borodin, Alexander, SYMPHONY NO. 2 IN B MINOR IN FULL SCORE. Rescored after its disastrous debut, the four movements offer a unified construction of dramatic contrasts in mood, color, and tempo. A beloved example of Russian nationalist music of the Romantic period. viii+152pp. 9 x 12. 0-486-44120-2

Brahms, Johannes, COMPLETE CONCERTI IN FULL SCORE. Piano Concertos Nos. 1 and 2; Violin Concerto, Op. 77; Concerto for Violin and Cello, Op. 102. Definitive Breitkopf & Härtel edition. 352pp. 9⅜ x 12¼. 0-486-24170-X

Brahms, Johannes, COMPLETE SYMPHONIES. Full orchestral scores in one volume. No. 1 in C Minor, Op. 68; No. 2 in D Major, Op. 73; No. 3 in F Major, Op. 90; and No. 4 in E Minor, Op. 98. Reproduced from definitive Vienna Gesellschaft der Musikfreunde edition. Study score. 344pp. 9 x 12. 0-486-23053-8

Brahms, Johannes, THREE ORCHESTRAL WORKS IN FULL SCORE: Academic Festival Overture, Tragic Overture and Variations on a Theme by Joseph Haydn. Reproduced from the authoritative Breitkopf & Härtel edition three of Brahms's great orchestral favorites. Editor's commentary in German and English. 112pp. 9⅜ x 12¼. 0-486-24637-X

Chopin, Frédéric, THE PIANO CONCERTOS IN FULL SCORE. The authoritative Breitkopf & Härtel full-score edition in one volume; Piano Concertos No. 1 in E Minor and No. 2 in F Minor. 176pp. 9 x 12. 0-486-25835-1

Corelli, Arcangelo, COMPLETE CONCERTI GROSSI IN FULL SCORE. All 12 concerti in the famous late nineteenth-century edition prepared by violinist Joseph Joachim and musicologist Friedrich Chrysander. 240pp. 8⅜ x 11¼. 0-486-25606-5

Debussy, Claude, THREE GREAT ORCHESTRAL WORKS IN FULL SCORE. Three of the Impressionist's most-recorded, most-performed favorites: *Prélude à l'Après-midi d'un Faune, Nocturnes,* and *La Mer.* Reprinted from early French editions. 279pp. 9 x 12. 0-486-24441-5

Dvořák, Antonín, SERENADE NO. 1, OP. 22, AND SERENADE NO. 2, OP. 44, IN FULL SCORE. Two works typified by elegance of form, intense harmony, rhythmic variety, and uninhibited emotionalism. 96pp. 9 x 12. 0-486-41895-2

Dvořák, Antonín, SYMPHONY NO. 8 IN G MAJOR, OP. 88, SYMPHONY NO. 9 IN E MINOR, OP. 95 ("NEW WORLD") IN FULL SCORE. Two celebrated symphonies by the great Czech composer, the Eighth and the immensely popular Ninth, "From the New World," in one volume. 272pp. 9 x 12. 0-486-24749-X

Elgar, Edward, CELLO CONCERTO IN E MINOR, OP. 85, IN FULL SCORE. A tour de force for any cellist, this frequently performed work is widely regarded as an elegy for a lost world. Melodic and evocative, it exhibits a remarkable scope, ranging from tragic passion to buoyant optimism. Reproduced from an authoritative source. 112pp. 8⅜ x 11. 0-486-41896-0

Franck, César, SYMPHONY IN D MINOR IN FULL SCORE. Superb, authoritative edition of Franck's only symphony, an often-performed and recorded masterwork of late French romantic style. 160pp. 9 x 12. 0-486-25373-2

Handel, George Frideric, COMPLETE CONCERTI GROSSI IN FULL SCORE. Monumental Opus 6 Concerti Grossi, Opus 3 and "Alexander's Feast" Concerti Grossi—19 in all—reproduced from the most authoritative edition. 258pp. 9⅜ x 12¼. 0-486-24187-4

Handel, George Frideric, WATER MUSIC AND MUSIC FOR THE ROYAL FIREWORKS IN FULL SCORE. Full scores of two of the most popular Baroque orchestral works performed today—reprinted from the definitive Deutsche Handelgesellschaft edition. Total of 96pp. 8⅛ x 11. 0-486-25070-9

Haydn, Joseph, SYMPHONIES 88–92 IN FULL SCORE: The Haydn Society Edition. Full score of symphonies Nos. 88 through 92. Large, readable noteheads, ample margins for fingerings, etc., and extensive Editor's Commentary. 304pp. 9 x 12. (Available in U.S. only) 0-486-24445-8

Mahler, Gustav, DAS LIED VON DER ERDE IN FULL SCORE. Mahler's masterpiece, a fusion of song and symphony, reprinted from the original 1912 Universal Edition. English translations of song texts. 160pp. 9 x 12. 0-486-25657-X

Mahler, Gustav, SYMPHONIES NOS. 1 AND 2 IN FULL SCORE. Unabridged, authoritative Austrian editions of Symphony No. 1 in D Major ("Titan") and Symphony No. 2 in C Minor ("Resurrection"). 384pp. 8⅛ x 11. 0-486-25473-9

Mahler, Gustav, SYMPHONIES NOS. 3 AND 4 IN FULL SCORE. Two brilliantly contrasting masterworks—one scored for a massive ensemble, the other for small orchestra and soloist—reprinted from authoritative Viennese editions. 368pp. 9⅜ x 12¼. 0-486-26166-2

Mahler, Gustav, SYMPHONY NO. 8 IN FULL SCORE. Authoritative edition of massive, complex "Symphony of a Thousand." Scored for orchestra, eight solo voices, double chorus, boys' choir and organ. Reprint of Izdatel'stvo "Muzyka," Moscow, edition. Translation of texts. 272pp. 9⅜ x 12¼. 0-486-26022-4

Mendelssohn, Felix, MAJOR ORCHESTRAL WORKS IN FULL SCORE. Considered to be Mendelssohn's finest orchestral works, here in one volume are the complete *Midsummer Night's Dream; Hebrides Overture; Calm Sea and Prosperous Voyage Overture;* Symphony No. 3 in A ("Scottish"); and Symphony No. 4 in A ("Italian"). Breitkopf & Härtel edition. Study score. 406pp. 9 x 12. 0-486-23184-4

*Available from your music dealer or write for **free** Music Catalog to*
Dover Publications, Inc., Dept. MUBI, 31 East 2nd Street, Mineola, NY 11501
*Visit us online at **www.doverpublications.com***